Dolly: A Comic Opera in One Act – Primary Source Edition

Adolphe Adam

"DOLLY."

A Comic Opera,
IN ONE ACT.

THE MUSIC BY ADOLPHE ADAM.

THIS VERSION OF THE LIBRETTO HAS BEEN
ESPECIALLY ADAPTED FOR PERFORMANCE
ON THE ENGLISH STAGE.

THOMAS HALES LACY,
89, STRAND,
(Opposite Southampton Street, Covent Garden,)
LONDON.

First performed at the Theatre Royal, Cork,
on Wednesday, the 26th day of December, 1860.

Characters.

CORNELIUS (*a Toy-maker in Nuremberg*) Mr. E. D. Corri.

JONATHAN (*his Son*) .... Mr. Bentley.

FRANZ MILLAR (*Nephew and Appren-*
tice of Cornelius) .... Mr. Charles Durand.

DOROTHY (*a young Milliner*) .... Madame Rudersdorff.

Scene.—THE HOUSE OF CORNELIUS IN
NUREMBERG.

PERIOD.—1780.

"DOLLY."

SCENE.—*The Back Shop of Cornelius. It is encumbered with dolls, drums, guns, trumpets, and with all sorts of toys, which hang upon the walls; door at the back, L. C., opening on the top of the staircase; a large fireplace, C.; and window, R.; closet door, L. 1 E.: door of Franz's chamber, R. 2 E.; an old oak chest; lamp alight on table, L.*

Enter CORNELIUS *and* MILLAR *from door,* L. C.—MILLAR *carries a light.*

CORN. (*pushing* MILLAR *before him*) Go along! The shop is closed, and 'tis 8 o'clock; so go to bed, and hold your candle straight.

MILLAR. (*with the candlestick in his hand*) But—uncle——

CORN. But—Jackanapes, you know I never allow any argument—it excites and worries me. There, get along! —I'm your master, and it is your duty to obey me. You're the most ungrateful young rascal in existence.— Don't I lodge you—board you—clothe you—although you don't possess a kreutzer in the world?

MILLAR. If I have not a kreutzer, it is because you have pocketed all that I should have.

CORN. (*angrily*) What?

MILLAR. All the little fortune my father left me was in a cash box, which *you* have taken such precious good care of, that I've never seen it.

CORN. Nephew—you forget that I am your uncle!

MILLAR. On the contrary, I am not likely to forget it, and without wishing to reproach you, I beg to say, that if you do lodge me—if you do clothe me, it is, because, you dare not expose me in this cold climate, in the original costume of Adam.

CORN. Is this, then, my recompense, after having worked, body and soul, to make you one of the cleverest workmen in Nuremberg?

MILLAR. There's not much merit in that, for I am useful to you in the manufacture of your mechanical toys, and dancing dolls, and self-acting young ladies——

CORN. Hold your tongue, sir! Go to bed, and mind you carry the candle straight.

MILLAR. Go to bed without supper, during the Carnival, too!

CORN. I sup abroad with friends. That is a sufficient reason.

MILLAR. (*aside*) But that's not a sufficient reason for my stomach.

CORN. My son Jonathan accompanies me——sweet cherub!

MILLAR. (*aside*) A stupid young pup!

CORN. (*impatiently*) Go to bed, I say! you'll sleep all the better for having no supper. No fear of the nightmare, I should say.

MILLAR. Good night, dear uncle; I wish you a good appetite for your supper. (*aside*) I hope it may choke you.

CORN. What did you say?

MILLAR. Nothing; only that you are so fond of a joke.

CORN. Psha! you know I hate a joke, and I hate flattery and humbug. Go in, I shall lock your door that you may not be tempted to make one amongst the fools at the Carnival.

MILLAR. Oh, uncle, you are welcome to do so. (*aside*) For all that, my Mephistophiles dress for the masked ball is ready in my room, and as I have another key for my door, you may lock me up as much as you like.

Exit MILLAR, R. 2 E.

CORN. (*speaking to* MILLAR *inside*) Mind! be at work to-morrow before day, if not, there'll be no breakfast for you.

MILLAR. (*inside*) Thank you, uncle. I hope you will amuse yourself.

CORNELIUS *locks the door and puts key in his pocket.*

CORN. (*alone*) There! He's safe for the night. My dear Jonathan is dressing up stairs, and I am here alone. (*he bolts the door at back*) Nobody can interrupt me! and I may devote a few moments to my great work. (CORNE- LIUS *opens mysteriously the door of the closet,* L. 1 E. *and takes out a doll the size of life—it is clothed in an elegant female costume, and covered with a long veil, and is seated in a large chair on castors*) There's my masterpiece! The eighth wonder of the world—my miraculous doll! What do I say? Doll! *No*—a living creature! When I say living—I mean all but living: but like a new Prome- theus, I will endow it with the vital spark. I will give it motion—speech. (*pointing to a book which is on the table to the right*) Thanks to this book, " The Treasure of Magic," (*sitting at the table and opening the book*) Let me see : page 117. (*reading*) " The person who would achieve this great work, must choose a dark winter's night, when the rain pours, and the wind howls, and the thunder roars, and the lightning flashes, and the hail rattles." Good gracious! One must have all the foul weather in the almanack to- gether. (*reads*) " The operator must then pronounce these three cabalistic words"——But, unfortunately, this is one of those abominably fine nights when there isn't a cloud in the sky. Well, one must have patience, we shall have dreadful bad weather if we wait for it : for I've always remarked that it's sure to come some time or another. (*addressing the doll*) Then, oh! doll! thou shalt have life, thou shalt have more, thou shalt talk—not too much though—and I shall have created for my son Jonathan a wife, in whom, grace, beauty, and innocence should be combined.

Song.

For many years my dream has been
    To give unto my darling boy,
A wife, of such perfections, queen
    Might yield him bliss without alloy.
I want her neither proud or mighty,
    But of a temper soft and sweet;
Her humour gay, yet far from flighty,
    All swains she with contempt should treat.

A girl who does not know to scold,
   To scold,
   To scold!
   But—hold!

But one with such a form and heart,
She must be made by rules of art.
   That well I know
   What did I do?
I made a girl by rules of art,
   By rules of art!

Of virtues numberless possessed,
 Adorned with ev'ry charm and grace.
She loves her home of all the best,
 And deems like it no other place.
She flies from ev'ry gay attraction:
 A ball can ne'er disturb her sleep,
Most prudent, wise, in ev'ry action,
 She'll e'en a secret closely keep ;
But, more than that, she will not chat,
   Not chat,
   Not chat!
   But—that—

Can not be had, with form and heart,
 Unless produced by rules of art.
   Indeed 'tis true,
   What did I do?
I made a girl by rules of art.
   By rules of art !

JONA. (*knocking outside*, L. C.) Papa, are you ready?
CORN. 'Tis Jonathan! (*calling loudly*) Yes, my darling.
(*to himself*) Quick, let me hide the figure. I do not wish
him to see her yet; her beauty might disturb his young
heart. (*he pushes the* DOLL *into the closet*, L.)
JONA. (*outside*) Papa!
CORN. (*shutting the door of the closet*) Yes, yes—coming.
Ah! and my book of magic—there! (*he puts it into the
chest*) Do not be impatient, my boy; here I am. (*he opens
the door*, L. C., *at the back*)

Enter JONATHAN, L. C.

JONA. (*entering*) Good gracious, papa, why do you always lock yourself up? One would think that you were coining false money.

CORN. Hush! Suppose any of the neighbours overheard you. Already my rivals in trade, jealous of my triumphs, accuse me of sorcery.

JONA. Well, papa, it is because you make such wonderful toys—birds that sing—dogs that bark—lambs that bah—even I myself——

CORN. (*astonished*) How, yourself!

JONA. I mean, that even I, sometimes ask, "Is papa indeed a wizard or a sorcerer. Is it possible that he has made any compact with the old toymaker, below."

CORN. (*putting his hand quickly on* JONATHAN'S *mouth*) Hush! What you've said might hang me, and you would not wish to see the author of your being hung, like a black doll, over his own door.

JONA. Oh, no, papa! I'd rather they'd hang you anywhere else!

CORN. (*aside*) Delightful candour! Come, are you ready, my boy? You know it's Carnival time, and we sup with our friend Vanlour.

JONA. Heigho! I don't care for supper.

CORN. Not care for supper! Bless me, what is the matter with you—you don't look well. Have you any uneasiness—any secret sorrow, my dear boy?

JONA. (*weeping*) Yes, papa!

CORN. (*sitting to the left*) Ah! Come here; sit on my knee, (*he takes him on his knee*) and confide to papa the grief that oppresses you.

JONA. Oh, papa! I am so sad. I want something to love, to caress—to cuddle!

CORN. Cuddle your father, my sweet cherub.

JONA. No! something—something fresh, and pretty— not like you. You know I shall be eighteen next spring, and my heart (*rising briskly*) wants a companion.

CORN. A companion! I have thought of this, Jonathan.

JONA. (*joyfully*) Oh, how jolly! Is she fair or dark? Are her eyes black or blue? When may I be married?

CORN. (*confidentially*) That depends on the weather.

JONA. (*astonished*) On the weather?

CORN. To-morrow, perhaps, if the barometer be favourable.

JONA. To-morrow?

CORN. Or next week.

JONA. Oh, dear papa, try to make it to-morrow! What is her name?

CORN. I have called her " Dolly."

JONA. You know her, then?

CORN. I know her as if she had been the work of these hands. But we shall be late—let us go.

JONA. (*at the window*) The sky is getting overcast, the wind begins to blow, and the rain patters against the windows.

CORN. (*with hope*) Indeed? (*taking* JONATHAN's *hands*) Ah! that may hasten your marriage!

JONA. What, the rain?

CORN. (*mysteriously*) Yes; with a little thunder and lightning.

JONA. (*amazed*) I do not understand you!

CORN. Never mind. Let us go. (*calling at the door*, R.) Millar! Millar! We are going! The idle rascal is already asleep.

JONA. (*calling at the door*) Cousin Millar, we are going to amuse ourselves. Good night!

(CORNELIUS *and* JONATHAN *exit at back*, L. C.—*when they are gone*, MILLAR *enters*, R. *door, wearing a costume of* MEPHISTOPHELES—*his face is half masked*)

MILLAR. (*alone—he takes off his mask, which he puts into his pocket*) Ah! my old knave of an uncle, you think I am going to bed at sparrow time in the Carnival, and without a morsel of supper—ha, ha, ha! You fancy I shall have no companion but my pillow. Oh very likely! not quite such a simpleton as that! I mean to enjoy myself in your absence according to a little plan of my own. In the first place I shall have a nice little supper here, with my dear Dolly, a charming little milliner, whom I expect every moment. After supper we go together to the masked ball, where we will fling ourselves madly into the whirlwind of the waltz. Ah! well, if we

have not riches, we have youth and light hearts to enjoy
life.

Song.

Yes, youth is life's treasure,
In joy and pleasure.
What is like the pow'r,
Which ev'ry hour
Is youth's gay dow'r.
When fond expectation
Sends in quick rotation,
Ev'ry beating pulse
With renew'd impulse?
All the week creeps sad and slowly,
By a scolding master watch'd,
And each hour in melancholy
Seems but by its hardships match'd.
My heart still 'gainst this fate so tearful
Comfort contrives,
When with her loving mien so cheerful,
Dorothy arrives.
Ah, cruel tutor, scold and cry,
More happy far than you am I.
For, for—ah! youth is, &c.

A sweet girl my heart possesses,
And her love to me confesses;
She's my soul, my pride, my life,
And to call her soon my wife,
Is the thought, which ever present
Day and night, me long has sought,
Making labour sweet and pleasant,
But alas! we both have nought.
Well, well, well, well!
Most certainly, this shall not make me sad,
Perhaps some day we shall be rich, for who can tell?
And while we wait, our love shall make us glad.

DOROTHY *outside*, L. C., *claps her hands three times.*

MILLAR. (*goes to door*, L. C.) Is that you, Dolly, dear?
DOR. (*outside*) Franz, why don't you light me up stairs?
MILLAR. (*speaking at door*) I beg your pardon. I

thought you might have come up by the light of your eyes (*takes lamp from table, returns to door, and lights in* DOROTHY, L. C., *who enters, enveloped in a cloak*)

Duet.—MILLAR *and* DOROTHY.

I am here!
I am here!

MILLAR }
and }   'Tis my dearest!
DOR. }   Thou appearest!
I see thee, oh, what pleasure!
Care and dread
Now have fled!
To me, my life's best treasure,
A kind fate thee has led.

DOR. (*looking at* MILLAR)
I see you're ready with your costume.

MILLAR. And you, my Dolly, what is yours?
How! What?

(*taking off her cloak, and surprised*)

DOR.   Yes, you will scold me, I presume.
MILLAR. But really I don't understand.
DOR.   If you will list, you'll comprehend.

Through all the week, with pleasure
I laboured day and night,
And gained a little treasure,
Which buy a dress well might;
But there came to me a poor creature,
In her arms her famished child—
Grief, despair, in every feature—
Asked me for bread, for pity mild.
So I gave all—gave all I had!
Ah! pardon me, for 'twas too sad!

MILLAR. What! I should scold? That would be fine!
Thou darling mine!
To make you good and merciful,
Some must, alas! be sorrowful.
If you have naught,
Or next to naught,
How blessed 'tis to find a way
In which some good bestow you may.

together) To make you good and merciful
                       Some must, &c.

MILLAR. Well, then we must give up the ball,
       And will instead of that with supper be contented.

DOR. Most vexing, still, it is for all,
       That to dance at the ball we thus should be prevented.

MILLAR. Never mind, Dolly dear, to fret there is no need,
       I throw away this disguise diabolic. (*his costume*)
       (*going towards his room*) Adieu! (*stopping*) But
            no (*reflecting*) this indeed will succeed.

DOR. (*surprised*) Well, what now?

MILLAR. (*to himself*) And why not?

DOR. (*laughing*) Pray what is this new frolic?

MILLAR. (*with solemnity*) A hope is dawning clear and
            bright,
       And after supper at the ball you'll dance to-night!

DOR.   How a disguise to find for me?

MILLAR.   I have it, dearest, here for thee.

DOR.   That suits me well!

MILLAR.   That you can wear.

DOR.   But where is it?

    (*he opens the door of the closet,* L. 1 E., *and shows*
     the DOLL)

MILLAR.   Come and look there.
       See, this doll has the dress you're wanting.

DOR.   Ah, just the thing! Oh, how enchanting!

MILLAR. You see, my darling, I was right!

DOR.   Now we shall dance, oh, what delight!

MILLAR. (*bowing ceremoniously*) For this waltz, will you
            your hand confer?

DOR. (*with a deep curtsey*) So much honour I scarce
            merit, sir.

together) There's nothing changed, oh, what delight!
  Now, after supper, gay and bright,
  We'll to the ball in rapid flight.
  Then we shall dance through all the night,
  To sounds of violin—flute and horn;
  We'll polk and waltz till break of morn.

Love gaily gives a counsel, thus:
" Hasten, ere youthtime vanish does.
Take care, take care! there's but one time to dance;
When winter comes there is no chance :
So hasten, and your youth enhance.
        Take care, take care,
  There's but springtime to dance !"
      Tra, la, la, la, la, la, la, la !   (*both dance*)

MILLAR. It is getting late—quick—quick, Dolly; go and dress yourself here in this little closet.

DOR. (*resisting a little*) But——

MILLAR. (*conducting her there*) Quick,—quick !

          DOROTHY *enters closet,* L. 1 R.

MILLAR. (*alone*) While Dolly is at her toilette I will lay the cloth for supper——(*the rain is heard beating against the windows*) Hallo ! can that be rain ? (*going to window ; laying table while he speaks*) Ah ! here's a change of weather ?—How it blows and rains—it will quite spoil the Carnival—(*thunder and lightning*) Lord, we're going to have a storm—Wasn't that a flash of lightning?—Ah !—there's thunder—What ill-luck—on this night too: but it may clear off by the time we've had supper: if it don't we can take a coach—it will be only going without dinner three days next week. (*whilst speaking he has placed the table in the middle of the stage;* VOICES *outside,* L. C., *he stops alarmed*) Good gracious ! somebody is coming up stairs——(*runs to door at back*) Oh, lord, 'tis my uncle and cousin——we are lost ! (*going to the door of the cabinet*) Dolly — Dolly — my uncle is on the staircase. (*he tries to open the door of the cabinet*) Come out—quickly !

DOR. (*inside*) Impossible !—I am undressed !

MILLAR. (*losing his presence of mind*) Dressed or undressed, you must come out. Heavens ! What shall I do ? (*taking the table he placed in the middle of the stage, and pushing it in every direction*) Under this table. Oh, no ! (*he puts the table back in its place*) In my room ? No—he will be sure to look there. Ah ! for an instant, till he goes to bed—up the chimney.

    He goes up the large chimney, C., *his legs now and then appearing.*

Enter JONATHAN *and* CORNELIUS, *both covered with snow, and chattering with cold, door* L. C.

JONA. Brr—brr—brr. How it snows and blows; I am drenched through clothes and skin to the bones.

CORN. The wind has nearly shaved my ears off.

JONA. But, papa, what an idea of yours to bundle off in such a hurry, just as I began to feel comfortable over a dish of stewed plums.

CORN. (*mysteriously*) The wind howls, and the thunder roars.

JONA. The greater reason that we should have remained.

CORN. (*solemnly*) The hail rattles, and lightning flashes. This grand commotion of the elements indicates the propitious hour when the triumph of my art will be accomplished.

JONA. Hold, papa! I venerate you, as you are the author of my existence——

CORN. Beloved offspring! (*embraces him*)

JONA. But for some time, I have had my suspicions, that you are——

CORN. What?

JONA. Slightly touched—here. (*touches his forehead*)

CORN. Touched—eh? Here? (*touches his forehead*)

JONA. There!

CORN. How?

JONA. Cracked!

CORN. (*with exaltation*) Cracked! Cracked! Then I suppose Galileo was cracked? And Christopher Columbus, was he cracked? And all the other geniuses of the world, were they cracked? You shall see if I am cracked!

JONA. Papa, oh dear! you frighten me.

CORN. (*with an air of inspiration*) Jonathan! have you the courage to hear an astounding revelation?

JONA. (*trembling*) Oh! I don't know; but, if you wish it—How cold I am, brr——Stay, let me make a fire first. (*the legs of* MILLAR *are perceived in the chimney*—JONATHAN *placing the wood in the fireplace*) I don't know whether it is with fear or cold, but I tremble like an ass —'pon—a—leaf.

CORN. (*sits*) Know then, my son, that I, Master Cornelius, have fabricated a girl.

B

JONA. (*with the bellows in his hand*) A girl!

CORN. I—with these hands.

JONA. Gracious powers!

CORN. A damsel, beautiful as Venus, who wants nothing but life to be perfect.

JONA. (*naively*) That is wanting everything. But where is she?

CORN. There! (*he points to the door on the left*) in that closet. The moment has come, when, by the power of magic, I shall give animation to my wondrous piece of mechanism.

Propitious is the hour, for conjurations mystic,
So let me take this precious book, (*he takes the book out of the chest*)
For I must speak the words of purport cabalistic.

(*he opens the books and seeks for the words*)

Ah! here they are! they meet my dazzled look!

(*during this time* JONATHAN *puts the wood in the fire place and begins to light the fire*)

CORN. (*with great emphasis*) Crick! Crack! Crock!

(*at each one of these words* JONATHAN *lights a match, which he puts to the fire*)

Trio.—JONATHAN, CORNELIUS, and MILLAR.

MILLAR. (*jumping down from the chimney, having resumed his mask*)
Hold, ah, hold!

CORN. (*in the greatest fright, falling flat on the ground*)
What do I hear?

JONA. (*falling on his knees, in consternation*)
'Tis the devil!
What a horrible appearance!

CORN.   I dare not lift to him my eye!

MILLAR. (*aside*) As they now take me for the devil,
Both to frighten I will try.

CORN. *and* } 'Tis the devil, yes, the devil!
JONA.   } Ah! I dare not lift my eye.

MILLAR. (*solemnly to* CORNELIUS)
    Master Cornelius, upon me you have called,
      And wished me to appear.
    Satan left his abode, and hath your wish forestalled.
      He stands before thee here.
CORN. (*trembling and rising, but remaining on his knees*)
    But sir, I never called upon you, on mine honor!
MILLAR. You meant to be of life to a woman the donor.
CORN. (*getting up, aside to* JONATHAN)
        He knows all!
JONA. (*trembling behind* CORNELIUS)
        He knows all!
MILLAR.   Yes, I know all!
    (*laughing satanically*) If you would animate,
          And create
      Some lovely female being,
      Never more, as 'tis need,
         You'll succeed,
    If Satan's not agreeing,
      By jove, no, by jove,
    If Satan's not agreeing!
CORNELIUS and JONATHAN. (*shivering with fear*) If you
      would animate,

        And create, &c.

MILLAR. (*taking the hands of* CORNELIUS *and* JONATHAN,
    who show signs of the greatest horror and fright)
Your hands now both of you, into mine must be placing,
    United then are we.
That then the doll here her steps may be tracing,
    Loud repeat now with me.
(*in an imperative voice*) With my infernal power commanding.
CORNELIUS & JONATHAN. (*with trembling voices*) With an
    infernal power commanding.
MILLAR. Come now, appear before us standing.
    (CORNELIUS *and* JONATHAN *repeat the same words*)
MILLAR. Humble, and without choice.
        (CORNELIUS *and* JONATHAN *idem*)
MILLAR. Hear the call of my voice.
        (CORNELIUS *and* JONATHAN *idem*)

DOROTHY *appears at the door of the closet,* L.—*she is dressed like the doll, and covered with the long veil;* MILLAR *goes to meet* DOROTHY, *gives her his hand, and whispers quickly in her ear.*

JONA. (*leaping with joy to his father*)
   The creature walks! Oh, how delightful!
    Dear papa, give her to me!
CORN. My darling boy, she's thine most rightful.
    So be calm—I'll give her thee.
MILLAR. To talk she's able.
CORN. How strange it is!
MILLAR.   Oh, not a bit!
  For she's a girl, and from her birth
      To talk is fit.

       Aria.—DOROTHY.

DOR.   Where am I?
       Where am I?
      What enchantment!
       What delight
       To the sight,
    Is this soft and thrilling light.
       Blessed ray,
       That to-day,
   To sweet life has shewn the way.
       Yes, my heart,
       With a start
       Animated,
       Palpitated,
      Pulses flowing,
      Quickly glowing,
     Strange new-born desire
      Inspire.
 All these scenes around so gay delight me
    Ah! what happy spell
    Thus upon me fell!
 And what transports powerful and mighty,
    Coming from above
    Bid me live and love.

Yes, this influence, mystic, tender,
　Which fond hopes in me instils,
Must my life most envious render,
　While with joy my soul it fills.

Jona. (*leaping with delight*) A musical doll! Oh, papa, how beautifully she sings! The wife you have manufactured for me I love and adore! (*kissing* Dorothy's *hands with delight*) Unite us quickly, or I shall go mad.

Dor. (*aside, to* Millar) What does he mean?

Millar. (*aside*) Hush!

Corn. My dear son, it was for you I made her, and from this evening she is yours. She shall be your wife!

Jona. (*jumping about with joy*) Oh! how happy I shall be! (*kissing* Dorothy's *hands again*)

Dor. (*aside to* Millar) But I don't like this at all!

Millar (*aside to* Dor.) Be quiet!

Jona. (*to* Millar) What did she say to you?

Millar (*embarrassed*) She said..... (*aside*) I must try to send them away. (*aloud*) She says she is hungry.

Corn. Hungry! already?

Dor. (*forgetting herself*) I should think so. I have not yet dined.

Millar. (*making a sign that she is going to betray herself*) Hum!

Jona. (*laughing*) How funny! She has not dined since she came into the world.

Corn. But we have nothing in the house. Never mind, I'll call that idle fellow Millar, who does nothing but sleep, and send him to fetch something for supper. (*goes towards* Millar's *room*)

Millar. (*stopping him*) It is unnecessary. Am I not here?

Corn. (*embarrassed*) Oh! oh! Mr. hem! hem!—I must not abuse your kindness by employing you as a messenger.

Millar. Don't you think my power enables me to order up a supper on the instant?

Jona. Ah! I forgot!

Millar. (*in a solemn tone*) Go into the kitchen, and there you will find a supper ready.

Corn. (*a little frightened*) But——

MILLAR. (*extending his arm as if to charm* CORNELIUS) Obey me!

JONA. (*trembling*) Papa! he commands it! Will it be hot?

MILLAR. I should think so, coming direct from my own fireside.   *Exit* CORNELIUS *and* JONATHAN, L. C.

MILLAR. (*taking off his mask*) At last they are gone, Dolly.

DOR. Thank heaven!

MILLAR. What shall we do now?

DOR. I don't want to be the wife of that fool; and you must get me out of this scrape somehow or other.

MILLAR. Hum! We must fly! I can think of no other way.

DOR. In this dress?

MILLAR. It can't be helped now.

DOR. My advice is that we should confess all!

MILLAR. That would never do! My uncle would turn me out of doors, and never forgive me.

DOR. Hush! I have it, I have it!

MILLAR. What?

DOR. An idea—a plan by which we shall trick them finely. Go into your room, and take off that dress.

MILLAR. But——

DOR. No words—go in, and be ready to help me.

MILLAR. But what are you going to do?

DOR. (*pushing* MILLAR *towards his room*, R.) Never mind —go in, I say! (*she makes him go in, and shuts the door quickly*) Just in time! And now I'll see whether I can be a match for the old fool and the young one.

Enter CORNELIUS *with tray, in which are dishes*—JONATHAN *with bottles and glasses, door* L. C.

CORN. (*placing tray on the table*) The devil is a capital cook. There!

JONA. (*putting bottles down*) We shall sup like burgomasters. (*looking for* MILLAR) Hallo! where is the mysterious stranger gone?

DOR. He had some pressing business at the other end of the world, and he's just popped off through the chimney.

CORN. Well! I can't say I am sorry, for he made me very, very uncomfortable; but never mind him. Supper is quite ready. Let us sit down. (*all three sit down—* DOROTHY *in the middle—*CORNELIUS *helps* DOROTHY *to a dish*)

DOR. What's this? I don't like it. Eat it yourself. (*thrusts plate back to* CORNELIUS)

JONA. Try this chicken, my pretty darling.

DOR. Chicken! it isn't chicken—it's roast crow (*flings plate away*)

CORN. (*to himself*) Her temper is rather quick, and her taste rather nice.

JONA. (*helping her to some cake*) This conserve my charmer, may please you—sweet creatures must have sweet things (*tries to kiss* DOROTHY'S *hand— she slaps him*)

DOR. And great fools must have smart things. I don't want supper. I'm not hungry. I wish to sing, dance, and amuse myself.

CORN. How! What!

JONA. Oh! do, papa, let us amuse ourselves.

CORN. Well, well—as you will! but let us remove the supper.

DOR. That's easily done. There it goes! (*she raises the corners of the table cloth, and throws it and the supper out of the window*)

CORN. Gracious heaven! All my beautiful china is gone!

Trio.

CORN. (*furious*) Oh! heaven, with vexation
    I'm half mad indeed.
   No, on this occasion
    I did not succeed.

DOR.   Why all this vexation?
   I'm formed in this way,
    And all obligation
   At your feet I lay.

JONA.   Papa, this vexation,
   Oh, heaven allay!
    I'm all admiration
   For all that you say.

DOR.   Evermore ready,
    Eager and steady
    Does my heart gladly
     All perils meet.

And my hand lightly,
Insults most slightly,
Quickly and brightly,
    Know to defeat.
But we will never quarrel or wrangle,
    Though if perhaps
You would oppose some whim or fangle,
    Take care of slaps !
              For—for——

    (*All three together*)

Evermore ready,
Eager and steady,
Does my ⎫
Does her ⎬ heart gladly
    All perils meet.
And my ⎫
And her ⎬ hand lightly
Insults most slightly,
Quickly and brightly
    Know to defeat.

Dor. (*taking a drum and two little guns, which she gives
   to* Cornelius *and* Jonathan)
    You shall take these arms,
While this drum I'm beating.
There's no use retreating,
    War for me hath charms !
We will form a corps of rifles,
    You'll make splendid volunteers,
    Ready now, and have no fears !
Corn. Upon my word, with me she trifles !
Jona.   Do not refuse, papa, let's play.
Dor.   Keep silence in the ranks, obey !
Attentive be and silent,
             When I command
Do not even whisper,
             Move not a hand,
But each slighest gesture,
             Quickly obey,
All my footsteps follow,
             Do not delay.

Haste, march, quickly on,
Row, to-row, to-row.

(*to* CORNELIUS) Upright hold your head,
Outward turn your toes,
Do not be afraid,
Thus a soldier goes,
Day and night in future,
Thus pass your life,
If you do not obey me,
War to the knife.
Vow therefore, march on,
Row—to-row—to-row.

A happy life it is, sirs,
That you will lead;
Causes for amusement
You'll never need.
Of the drum you're tired?
Well, never mind!
Here I've got a trumpet;
Is not that kind?
List how merrily,
Tran ta ran taree.

Gaily breaks the sound
Through the night around!
But I promise ye,
Noisier ne'er I'll be.
Day and night in future,
Thus pass your life!
To the cheerful music
Of drum and fife.
Won't we happy be,
Tran ta ran taree!

CORN. (*furious*) Ah! 'tis too much;
This a woman is never!
JONA. Oh! yes, papa,
For I do love her more than ever.
CORN. This is no woman, 'tis a demon,
Yes, a demon 'tis indeed!

DOR.   Yes, you have said it, a demon tormenting,
        Of whom ne'er thou more canst be freed.
        Will all the night some new trouble inventing,
        Remain to punish thee for thy bold deed.

(running here and there, overturning and breaking all the toys, and always escaping CORNELIUS, *who runs after her)*

                I'll break,
                I'll make
        Such dreadful confusion!
        And turn everything upside down!
                I'll dare
                    To tear
        And smash all to pieces.
        Never caring for all your frowns!
        Your china, your glasses,
        Each plaything, each toy,
        Your statues, your brasses,
        To ruin I'll try;
        Not timid nor coy,
        Everything I'll destroy.

CORN. *(breathless, pursuing her)* Beware of my anger!
JONA. *(in despair)* Oh! pray cease this clangour.
DOR.   I laugh at the languor
        Of your idle wrath.
CORN. *(taking up a child's sword)*
        This weapon shall strike you!
JON. *(stopping his father)* Ah! this is alarming,
        Yet see, she is charming!
DOR.   I but laugh at you!
                I'll break,
                I'll make, &c.
COR. & JON.   She'll break,
                She'll make, &c.

*(*BERTHA, *just as* CORNELIUS *is on the point of catching her, turns over everything in her way, and throws herself into the closet on the left, which* JONATHAN *immediately shuts)*

    JONA. *(before the door in a dramatic attitude)* Oh, papa! pity, pity for my bride!

Enter MILLAR (*who has resumed his former dress*), R. *door.*

MILLAR. (*coming from his room and rubbing his eyes as if just awoke from sleep*) Oh, dear! oh, dear! what an uproar! what a row! (*as if astonished*) What! is it you, uncle? already returned!

CORN. (*aside to* JONA.) Franz! he must not suspect anything! (*loud and sharply*) What do you want?

MILLAR. I was sleeping like a top, when I was suddenly awakened——

CORN. You had no business to awake!

MILLAR. How could I help it? Who could sleep through such a noise of singing, dancing, drumming, fifing, smashing of everything, as if the devil had been giving an evening party here?

CORN. (*aside*) The devil! Hem! (*loud*) You don't know what you are saying! you are still asleep and dreaming!

MILLAR. (*pointing to the toys about the room*) Asleep! No, I'm wide awake. Were all these things knocked about in a dream?

CORN. Never mind. It's no affair of yours! Return to your bed!

MILLAR. But, uncle, allow me to observe——

CORN. To bed! instantly! to bed!

MILLAR. (*aside—pointing to closet*) She is in the closet.

CORN. Still here? (*to* MILLAR) Go in, or I shall kick you out of my house!

MILLAR. Kick me out! (*aside*) The very thing I wish.

CORN. And you shall take with you my malediction!

MILLAR. Thank you, uncle. What am I to do with it? Will you lend me a bag to carry it in?

CORN. Get away, you impudent dog! get away!

MILLAR. (*still stopping*) I'm going! (*aside*) I should think she ought to be ready——(*pointing to the door on the left*) the window of the closet looks on the garden.

JONA. Why don't you go, cousin?

CORN. Why don't you go?

MILLAR. (*quietly*) I am going! I'm going! (*aside*) A ladder, and she is safe! (*aloud, very quietly*) I am going, good gracious, I *am* going!

He goes out at the back, L. C.

CORN. (*returning to* JONATHAN, *with a very serious air*). Jonathan!

JONA. (*jumping up with fear*) Papa!

CORN. (*tragically*) Are we alone?

JONA. (*looking uneasily around him*) Well, it seems so, papa.

CORN. Jonathan! The wife which I have manufactured for you is——

JONA. What, papa?

CORN. A demon!

JONA. Oh, papa! Don't.

CORN. She has more of the devil in her than any woman I ever met—she's animated by Satan.

JONA. Do you think so?

CORN. I fear it! She will destroy my house, she will be the ruin of thy youth, and the shame of my grey hairs!

JONA. (*uneasily*) Well, papa?

CORN. Well, an awful idea crosses my brain!

JONA. You frighten me!

CORN. Does not the sculptor break his statue, if he is not satisfied with his work?

JONA. Certainly.

CORN. Does not the painter destroy the canvas which caricatures the ideal of his dreams?

JONA. Of course.

CORN. Then, the die is cast!

JONA, (*with despair*) What, papa? What would you do? You know I love her.

CORN. Don't grieve for her, Jonathan, I will soon make another for you, my boy.

JONA. Exactly like her?

CORN. Oh, no! not like her, I hope. One of a much better quality, and finer workmanship. This one's fate is decided! (*he listens at the door of the closet*) She is there, alone—the deed must be done at once! Give me the light! (*he takes a hammer*) Or rather, no, I'll have no light! (*he enters the closet*)

JONA. (*alone, listening, trembling*) Oh dear, how my legs shake! I feel my hair bristling on my head! Papa, papa! mercy!

Cornelius re-enters, pale and agitated.

Is is done already?

CORN. (*with the greatest emotion*) Hush! she was sleeping in her chair—I raised my hand and struck the blow! at the instant, the window was opened violently, and I beheld a white figure gliding from it into the garden.

JONA. Ah! depend upon it, 'twas her spirit!

CORN. A wicked spirit, I've no doubt, for I heard shouts of feminine laughter outside, and it was Satan who was laughing to have got back his property!

Enter MILLAR cautiously at the back, L. C., shaking his fist, and laughing at CORNELIUS and JONATHAN.

MILLAR. (*aside*) Ah! I have you now! (*coughing aloud*) Hum! hum!

CORN. (*frightened*) Ah!

JONA. (*frightened*) Oh!

CORN. (*furiously*) You again? What is it? What do you want? What business have you coming here to play the spy?

MILLAR. (*pretending to be embarassed*) My dear uncle, I wish to make a confession to you.

CORN. Then be quick about it!

MILLAR. You know, my good uncle, I have the fault of being very curious—

CORN. That's only one of your faults! Proceed!

MILLAR. Well, that closet which you kept always so carefully locked (*pointing to the closet*) excited my curiosity.

CORN. (*aside*) Heavens! what's coming now?

MILLAR. This evening you forgot the key in the door there, and during your absence, 1 regret it sincerely, dear uncle, I entered the closet—

CORN. You entered it—and I—

MILLAR. (*pretending to weep*) Oh! that was nothing, but I'll confess all! That doll, which you made in secret—what a pretty thing it was!—I saw it, I admired it—I touched it, and lifted it, but in doing so it slipped from my awkward hands! and was broken.

JONA. and CORN. (*astonished*) Broken!

MILLAR. (*still pretending to weep*) Yes, dear uncle, in

a thousand pieces, and I was in despair, but I thought
if I could gain a little time before making this confession,
I might be able to soften your anger—so as deceive you
until to-morrow, in case, on your returning home, you
should look into the closet, I put in place of your masterpiece of arts, a masterpiece of nature—a pretty little girl,
whom I love!

Corn. (*aside, staggering*) Great heaven! (*he falls into*
Jonathan's *arms, who tries in vain to sustain him*)

Millar. (*continuing*) The poor girl is there still a
prisoner, and I came to beg you to pardon us both, and
set her at liberty. (*he goes towards the closet as if to open
it*)

Corn. (*placing himself quickly before the door*)
          Away, stand back, away! stand back.

Millar. (*aside*) I laugh to see them on the rack.

Corn. So you said that this girl was living.

Millar. Of course she's living! Why this misgiving?
     Let me take her away.

Corn. (*stopping him*)   From hence quick go!

Millar. But not without her!

Jona. ⎫
  and ⎬ I faint with fright, I see all black!
Corn. ⎭

(*together*)

Corn.   Heavens! I am dying,
                  And my anxious fear
              Sees the justice prying
                  Close to me, and near!
              Of a crime indicted,
                  That for vengeance calls.
              Ah! on me convicted
                  Penalty now falls!

Jona.   Heavens! I am dying,
                  And my anxious fear
              See the justice prying
                  Close to us, and near!
              Of a crime indicted,
                  That for vengeance calls.
              Ah! on us convicted.
                  Penalty now falls!

MILLAR. (*laughing—aside*) Look, with fright he's dying,
   And with anxious fear
  Sees the justice prying
   Close to him, and near!
  Of a crime indicted,
   That for vengeance calls,
  Thinks on him convicted,
   Penalty now falls!

 (*approaching the closet*) This lasts too long, and
  patient I'll no more be.
 (*calling*) So come, Dorothy!
CORN. (*greatly frightened*) Be quiet, I implore thee!
MILLAR. To fetch her out, I have the right.
CORN. (*opposing* MILLAR)   No, no!
JONA. (*to* CORNELIUS) If thou yield'st, death is before thee!

   (*march of the night watch heard outside*)

MILLAR. Ah! I hear the watch of the night!
  They will sure aid me to discover
  This mystery, and lift the cover
  Of my suspicions.
CORN. (*with terror*) Oh, heavens!
MILLAR. (*going to the window*) I'll call!
CORN.
 and } (*holding him back*) Ah, hold! ah, hold! have
JONA. pity on thy kindred!
CORN. (*solemnly*) If you will swear to me, with vows
   most solemn, sacred,
  That you will nevermore this secret seek to know—
  That you will far away from here this instant go;
  Then everything that you demand,
  I vow I'll give into your hand.
MILLAR. I consent, but on the sole condition,
  That you my father's gold return!
JONA. Ah, give it him, and think of our position!
CORN. Ten thousand crowns! His mad demand I spurn!
MILLAR. Well, then, the watch I'll call hither.
JONA. Papa, obey, or he'll go thither.
  Ah, this expedient can save us alone.
CORN. I see't, alas! All hope is gone!
 (*gives* MILLAR *a cash box, which he takes out of the chest*)

MILLAR. (*joyfully, and calling out*) Now, Dorothy, quickly
   come to me,
  The game we've won—thanks to thee!

   Enter DOROTHY, *dressed as at first, door* L. C.

JONA. (*showing her to* CORNELIUS, *with astonishment*)
  Oh, papa! look, oh, look! we are cheated!
CORN. Eh?—Ah!—What!
JONA.   'Tis the Doll!
CORN. (*angrily to* MILLAR)   Ah, you rake!
  Oh, this trick will a fool of me make!
DOR. We played a game in which we've won the stake!
       (*showing the cash box*)
MILLAR. I've won a bride, and have your plans defeated!
       (*embracing* DOROTHY)
DOR. May I hope that you will honor my bridal day
  With your charming presence, cheerful and gay?
  Thus, yourselves shall witness, that Doll so wild,
  Turned by love most potent—good, sweet, and mild!
CORN. *and* JONA. Confounded be their treachery!
    If wrath could slay,
    Mine would to-day!
   Still we both must smile
   With careful guile!

DOR. }
MILLAR. } Day and night, in future, we'll pass this life,
  As a loving husband, and tender wife,
   Won't we happy be,
   Tran, taran, taree!

𝕮urtain.

Printed by Thomas Scott, Warwick Court, Holborn.

librariessellers

Mrs. Crowe's Play—The Cruel Kindness, 6d.

The Rev. Dr. BELLOWS'S DEFENCE OF THE STAGE,

With a Pre

CPSIA information can be obtained at www.ICGtesting.com
Printed in the USA
BVOW07s0111220715

409751BV00002BA/3/P